BOOK OF DOG

ALSO BY CLEOPATRA MATHIS

Aerial View of Louisiana (1980)

The Bottom Land (1983)

Guardian (1995)

What to Tip the Boatman? (2001)

White Sea (2005)

BOOK OF DOG

Poems

Cleopatra Mathis

Sarabande Books
LOUISVILLE, KENTUCKY

Managing Editor
Sarabande Books, Inc.
2234 Dundee Road, Suite 200
Louisville, KY 40205

Library of Congress Cataloging-in-Publication Data

Mathis, Cleopatra, 1947–
  Book of dog : poems / Cleopatra Mathis.
     p. cm.
  Includes bibliographical references and index.
  ISBN 978-1-936747-47-4 (pbk. : alk. paper)
  I. Title.
  PS3563.A8363B66 2013
  811'.54—dc23
                                  2012029732

Cover painting by Louise Hamlin.
Cover and text design by Kirkby Gann Tittle.

Manufactured in Canada.
This book is printed on acid-free paper.

Sarabande Books is a nonprofit literary organization.

The Kentucky Arts Council, the state arts agency, supports Sarabande Books with state tax dollars and federal funding from the National Endowment for the Arts.

For Ellen Bryant Voigt

"We live in a cage of light an amazing cage
Animals animals without end"
—Ikkyū

Contents

I. Canis

Answer

When she came back from walking the dogs
he would not look at her. Fast in his place on the couch
he said whatever he said
without urgency: she was like any other distraction.
The set of his jaw, his lips,
reminded her of a prisoner, of something trapped,
or of the very old—anyone consigned to waiting
and who has chosen to obey. Meanwhile, between them
a hole had been dug, immense,
all their words thrown in there,
irretrievable. Or mangled,
torn from their real meanings or intent, just given over
to *why should it matter now?* And for her, now,
replaced by the plain language of the dogs,
who in a few syllables have everything to say.

Ants Want My Yellow Moth

The one that came to me out of the sea, perfect
serrated edges of its six wings,
each seamless with tiny yellow feathers,
the two bright center ones with fake black eyes
pretending sight. Even drowned,
the wings held tight, a simple knot at the top
attaching them to the black worm of the body.
What fragile stitchery the tide held up,
carrying it in on a wave. I took it to my desk,
arranged it so as to see the colors as they dried,
the veins rising, shuddering with my breath.

But now, this ant has found its way
under my immaculate shack and climbed the pilings,
through gaps in the floorboards to one leg
of my writing table, and up that to the surface
plane of three cracked boards, where it scurries
to the moth: my creature.
Pulled from the sea with my own hands—mine, I think,
because I believe my very will can save it.

Song of If-Only

If only the bird had been alive, not something dead
delivered onto sand; and not this packed cold sand,
where nothing moves even slightly, no blow-holes,
no scurrying things, and if only the shore birds'
seaweed nests, that little piping, hadn't been smothered
by a freak spring tide. Now the plovers must begin again:
eggs and hatching, the mothers' fake writhing
when they see me, squawking and dragging their wings
to save their chicks. Oh save me

from the whole painstaking work of early June—
this blowing fifty degrees, no sand bed of heat
in some dune bowl's hollow, no love,
and on this outer beach Euphoria
just the name of the shack I want in this driving rain.
And if only it would stop, shut itself up for good—
this off-key *if only* that goes on singing,
like some deranged child, repeating.

Dead Fox

We pretended to know nothing about it.
I withdrew to childhood training: stay out
of swampy undergrowth, choked edges.
This was around the time
we were too cruel to kill the mice we caught,
leaving them in the Have-a-Heart trap
under the sun-burning bramble of rugosa.
But moving up the trail, we caught a glimpse
right at the start: the fox just over the hillock
on the dune-side slope, spoiling
the grass-inscribed sand. Neither of us looked—
it seemed best to back away.
On the dune's steep side
we surveyed what we'd come for: ocean's
snaking blues beyond the meadow, the silvered
blade-like wands lying down. Lovely enough
to hold ourselves to that view.
But the currents of an odor wafted in and out,
until the sweep of smell grew wider, wilder.
The heat compounded, and ugliness
settled its cloud over us, profound as human speech,
although by then we were not speaking.

Chipmunk in the Pool

Chippy fallen in, little head bobbing,
and from the second floor, dark in their conversation,
she runs to rescue. No handy net to lift it out, no
chipmunk-sized anything, so she throws
her shirt, a raft of sorts to scamper on,
too heavy, too close—how could she not know this,
her usual way of jumping in before thinking—
and it flips, goes under.
The broom, she's calling now to the silent house,
bring me the broom.

The creature fights itself up, and she leans
to grab the baby belly and soaked heft,
pluck it out to the air where it gasps a little, chokes out
water from a gaping mouth. She massages with one finger
where the lungs might be. More droplets gurgle up;
mouth to mouth is needed
along with pumping. But she can't, not without
some small opening to blow through,
safe distance from her own mouth, which
has released a little drool, working in sympathy
as if she can convince this thing to be saved—
how hard can it be in the tame backyard pool?

And why can't he come out of the house
with some other idea, that tumbler of straws
plain on the kitchen counter; why
for God's sake, won't he come out and help?

Their Chamber

She was thinking of his explanation
as a kind of Möbius strip, circling
endlessly, seamlessly reversing and twisting
to reveal the underside, on-going words. Lost in it,
she reached down into the limited
rough space between the bed and the wall,
and her hand came up skinned, the top layer
from knuckle to wrist peeled away.
This was part of her usual vigilance—
He would spill something, lose something, and she'd
rush to wipe away, find the missing,
like this automatic retrieving of his sock—

Beaded with blood, she examined
the wide scrape in addition
to sunspots, moles, the wormy down-under,
raised-vein look of her skin. Another thing on her body
to heal outside, while inside
running through her, the ribbon of his words:
no, then *yes*, *yes*, and *no* again. Oh what did he want

and how could she manage to wait
for the circling to stop—
how could she keep still?

When She Spoke, He Closed His Eyes

So she tried to disappear, obliged
by his own disappearing, becoming
who she wasn't. *Not there* was not
who she was, and not *how* she was.
She could tiptoe out, he could be
relieved or (surprise!) come searching.
But how would that work
when he needed her to be there
in order to make her gone, disappeared
into *other*. What other? she thought, wondering
how to make herself into someone
absent, so she could be the one
he would welcome, wide-eyed, wanting
to hear whatever it was she had to say.

Labyrinthitis

1. *When it began*

First a fret in which everything changed.
By morning an underwater language
had overcome me.
When I tried to rise

my body said fall, and so I did.
My weighted hair, my head
turned me over. I could not hear him straight.
I was a doll with a mechanical box, the *Mama*

crying over and over, a dummy,
a dropped marionette.
Hold me, I said.
So sorry, he said.

2. *Not making sense of it*

If he was calling, I was too far under—
arm over arm
tangled in the heaving wave,

the body catching
the slap of stones,
swept through a passage.

The brain's sea in a little box
washed in, a spinning top
come to a stop. Tilted.

•

He was walking some inert shore.
Always the lifeguard, he used to say,
eyes fixed on the water.

3. *Nevertheless a common disorder*

Some infection in the water, a nastiness
washing through. At first an incidental ache,
then recurring, inflaming
the air-filled cavity of the middle ear—
who knows how it starts,

how it finds the inner ear,
a spiraling labyrinth,
the fluid-filled temporal bone
where two organs live: the embedded
nerves for hearing, or mis-hearing,
and, in a semicircle of canals, the home
for balance. Never

one without the other.
Somewhere in there should have been a marriage.

Canis

It was a small comment, wasn't it, about who they were
—that last year on the dunes when all the town talk
was of coyotes, prairie wolf in search of an ocean,

those footprints instead of rabbits' surrounding the shack
or half-sunk in the cranberry bog
just off the path. They heard the howling somewhere

behind their backs as they walked out past midnight,
singing at the top of their lungs:
abandon me, oh careless love—although they knew

the coyotes knew exactly where they were. No surprise
to either of them when they wailed unusually close
and loud on a moonless night after an argument,

this time a mean one about the dogs. For God's sake,
the dogs, how much trouble they were to him,
their feeding and whining and constant

need to go out, no matter how wet or cold. And so on
till silence set itself between them, holding stiff
as each turned away to bed. But the coyotes just outside

started up their merciless lament, as if
the entire genus called them, had bound the tribe together
in protest for their brothers. Hours they heard the keening,

both of them sleepless, that rising, falling
complaint in their ears—until he couldn't bear it, he said
I'm sorry, I can't do this anymore, and she in a rush

of understanding the exact suffering fit of it, jumped up
and closed the offending one window's
half-inch crack, and just like that

in the dead center of a moan, the coyotes
stopped their noise; what I mean to say is
the wind stopped making that heartbroken sound.

Interstice

1. Between Grief and Sorrow

Grief staggers around the house
some thief has emptied.
It wants to tell you everything
all over again; blame is the story
grief hammers, hammering until your leg shakes,
your right foot won't stop tapping.
It's a dance for the shaken,
strung out with waiting, and now look
who's back to guard the door:
grief's half-sister, dread.

2. The Coldest Weather

Young trees bend, white trunks slender enough
to spring back, softening the woods however they stand.
But in the bigger ones, you can hear
ice exacting its pull in the pines and spruce.
A pause, a sharp crack
and they snap, the whole tree
breaking away from the heartwood,
long tears of sapwood
going to pieces as they fall. Violent and brutal,
that was our winter. The ground deepened with waste.

3. In the Woods

Because there were no words he could hear,
I made myself mute, and because
the binding ice of another year

held the same branches down, they were dying,
and trying to free whatever green ones I could
was pointless. Still, I choose this task

for what it says about hiding and watching:
pulling at a dead limb releases a clatter,
and as I stand there,

dark surrounding trunks come alive
and leap away. The deer
is designed to resemble a tree,

and I only need take one brittle stick
to brittle bark and bang it to see everything plain—
the deer tearing through woods,

believing he is running for his life.

I Will Be Good

I will be good, I will wait
on the birds, the turkeys, the deer. I will provide
the black-oil seeds, dried corn
(the gold so shiny on snow), and I will not watch
the progressive stripping
of the slender ornamental cherry.
For the clumsy doves, I will use my hands
to dig out the scatter of thrown-out seed,
and even after the woodpecker fattens and preens,
I will render the suet, cool it and mold it,
and wade out to his old lone tree
to hang it free from other feeders.

As for my finches in their sullen coats of dun and ash,
fluffed feathers holding off the cold
but not the hardening weight of record snow,
what can I do but beg?
And when that icy knot of a creature
falls on my porch,
I will bring a hairdryer
and plug it into the outdoor socket, and I will cover
the bird with diffused, kind air.
I will warm the great outdoors
for the whole of January if I can.
I must be good, and I will see it
if a single breath stirs.

New Snow

Why now do I care to look—
though everything outlined in these woods
makes itself known: prints of a snowshoe hare,
long narrow pods in pairs, slightly dug-in at the heels
as they hop forward; the chipmunk's and vole's faint
gifted script, and one ribbon of something
curving out on the pond's blank surface.
All these have crossed the trail, never directly
forward, where my boots trudge right and left
like a one-man army dragging through the dead of white.

I know they watch—no animal trusts
what a human might pursue—as I watch
for their unmoving silence in the falling snow, their ways
drawing me through the narrow gaps the deer have made,
revealing the emptiness deeper in, and yes,
there it is: the old oak with a block carved out,
the wounded trunk already dead, shirred off.
And eye-level in that exact inner space, a lady's shoe:
satin tattered to its bones,
a pitted rhinestone fan on top, one scar of ruby red,
and jammed in the toe, a rock to keep the shape.
Why not black with rot by now, this bridal shoe in a tree
I couldn't find in the dense green and gold seasons,
when it mattered.

Essential Tremor

More white tendrils to free
from rotten snow and the clenched ground—
tulips you hope that time will turn green.
You claw the drifts

till your gloved fingers freeze.
You wonder what fat grubs might tend them,
what hatching consume them?

Anxiety has forged another weather.
You wake with the shakes,
a waver when you stand, a slipstream
of early light propelling you
out to the garden.

What a grip has got you,
what a prison you've assumed.

In Lent

Dead deer a week now by the snowy gate.
Do I have to watch it be eaten? Do I have to see
who comes first, who quarrels, who stays?

And there is the question of the night,
what flesh preferred by which creature—
what sinew and fat, the organs, the eyes.
These appetites: it's enough
to know the swoop and cut of wings
over the snarl of something leaping away.

Do I have to see the icy figure fused to the ground,
scrabbled snow, not lovely or deep,
but the surface of something spoiled?
By now the rib bones arch above it all,
unbroken light shining between them,
above the black cavity.

And I hear the crows, complaint, complaint
splitting the morning, hunched over the skull.
They know their offices.

Noise

We'd come so far, I kept saying.
I was full of myth, which is to say
full of an idea. The sea lent its own persuasion,
banging its way in. Listen, I said,
flying my music of need and want
into the ever-reaching sky.

But inside that artifice
there was shoving, and he saw it.
He lay down and closed his eyes.
In the sand's obliging hollow, an anodyne
in the shadow's varying whites,
he made himself flat
so as to bring the warm sun against the plane of his body.
The demanding wind would pass right over.

Over

The *slogging on* he called it,
a phrase that brings the mud in with it.
But if I limped around in one swollen, cracked shoe,
he had the other, and finally he let it fall,
like a thick book held high then slamming
flat against the floor. The dogs jumped
out of their languid sleep—maybe a signal they thought
to go outside, back down to the creek
where the big one likes to wade and the little one
drags her butt along the sloppy edge.
But no alarm in their regard, just a dazed moment
before they closed their eyes again. No barking,
in fact, no noise at all.

II. Book of Dog

Book of Dog

1.

All praise to the light on the wing
of the wasp fallen to the wood floor,
enough universe for the dog
waiting while you are away.
But as long as your body sits on the chair,
he's not worried
where you are and when you look up
from that far place, he returns
may I lick your hand—the sign
you give back in the glory
song of the one word:
his name in your mouth.

2.

The other one's roaming closer, a shy dog
after this morning's rudeness—
belly to the floor, head bent,
she's crawling
to your chair, remembering
not to bark. Does my breath still stink,
can I sleep in your bed? What if
I promise not to wake you,
rolling over scratching an itch.
Thump goes the tail on the wood floor.

Bless her everlasting guilt.
Bless her eye on you.

3.

In the book of dog, a few syllables contain the world,
and you own them. You dole out *car, home, sit,*
stay—for the sweet yelp, the whine.
But at *cookie,* the wet mouth seizes,
the low growl transforming *Give it to me*
Into *oh how I love you.* The pure
love we assign when the dog gets
what it wants. And when it doesn't,
that famously humble and contrived
looking the other way, studying the air—
the mote in the air—
the not wanting for anything, not saying
Oh you dear one with the meat, the bone, the biscuit,
come back, give it to me.

4.

Again the wolf before I wake.
I am walking near dawn, and yellow eyes flicker.
Where are my dogs? Lost in sleep.

Back in the morning, the dogs
tear apart their beloved toy. Poor dear,
I tell them, little thing is dead.
I can't put the stuffing back.
I've fed them their kibble, their bit of meat.
They eye me, unrelenting.

We go out in the fog the morning won't burn.
The dogs go wild with sniffing.
Noses down, they whine in circles
where something once stood,
where they last glimpsed him.
They can wait all day.
Hush, hush, I coax: he's long gone.
But you can't fool a dog—
no matter what,
they plan to bring him home.

5.

Daily the ruined rise out of snow.
The terrier spends hours dragging forth
whatever she uncovers, not clean bones
but dank, fur-covered—hooves still attached.

The snow is tending toward nothingness,
frozen water whose melting
goes jagged and sheer on the path.
And when you fail to feed the birds,
the finches go elsewhere, living without as they do.
The blameless reappear, that small scrambling.

So much springs back—
silence sweeps through, a voice in its breath:
Fearful one, when were you not beloved?

6.

Winter again: dogs on the floor,
their dream-whimpers, their licks.
Sleet on the window,
and the crippled one
pricks his ears, jerks
and rows his long thin legs.
Alaskan mix, he'd been a wolf,
so much like that one in photos you've seen,
the long snout held up in snow.
He's grown gaunt as they are, something in him
gone back—no longer your pet
loping through woods, white fur
in and out of the birches,
keeping pace those years you ran the road.
Once, he leapt on a squirrel,
one mean shake to death—
this dog whose every sign you thought
human in its love, not seeing
the work of transformation
and disguise.

7.

How will you do it all without him,
he asks with his eyes, steady as always
on your every shudder, the tremulous rise in your voice.
Any sign of dismay obliges him
to lay his head in your lap.

So when his body, bullied into change,
pushes him to fall down sideways,
his brain slipping its curiosity aside,
eyes and ears falling second to intuition,
and even danger seems an indifferent thing,
he will try to go to the woods, or any hidden place,
as if to an origin some instinct
has handed down, centuries
before the human generations of home.

When your back is turned,
he'll go find a rock, a fallen tree,
a clump of hemlock where he'll just lie down.
His dignity in the last breath brought on by night's cold,
or something strong and hungry, not malevolent—
This is what the dog wants.
The worst thing would be to frighten you.

8.

I'm drawn by the creaking—
time to bring the dead limbs down! A forked one
cracks, braced by a bough right over my head.
I screech, the little dog leaps—
oh the chugging engine of her heart,
tongue hanging out, red petal.
More, the terrier pants, all her dumb self quivering,
rolling, four legs swimming in the sunny air.
Clown dog, somersault queen of sticks.
This, it occurs to me, is funny—here I am,
lost in dog. I regard the big one
lying there, savoring in his masked way,
white angel ruffling. I look where he looks:
eyeing the wind in simple green, a spider of color
dotting the boughs. The black made more visible,
the dead more dead.

9.

What you say to the dog: no dying tonight!
Too soon, too cold, and his beloved snow
has come, a thick coat
glazing lashes and lids, the little pile of it
sitting on his nose. Black nose quivering,
held up for the fall. Turn your back
and he's pushing past the fence, the drifting
thigh high, the white grave of it:
what *is* it he sees swaddled in white?
And now the snow's biting,
bits so little they make a strobe in the air's
slanted theater, blind home,
where the dog wants to go.

•

You've seen that look in the very old—
a propelling forward as if without thinking,
or a thinking that has broken connection to what
it is the body's doing. The dog's not hearing:
no answer comes back, but no answer's withheld.

•

Stop whining, here's a cookie!
White hair, white light, a sigh of relenting
when he lets himself down.
One hip shudders, the other falls. Can this be pain
when the bed's so soft, hindquarters cushioned.
Too much saintliness

will wear us all down.
Mouth kisses everywhere,
even from the terrier, and the cats
come close with their sniffing regard.
The dog is made of heaven, dog's life chugs on.
His *going-on*, his *now,* needing to be
brought to a halt—and you not able to see
his eyes full of you
done with and gone.

10.

On the day he died, I went out to hit trees.
It had been a long winter with unforgiving winds,
too cold for snow, and the woods were knotted
with fallen limbs caught high above ground.
I swung with a stick, thrashing over my head
till the dead parts flew, cracking or flying back.
Some trees were broken off, jagged
around the heartwood, that dense central core.
I fought deeper in, careless
with branches three or four times my length, thicker
than my arm. I had to balance and dodge,
practiced in the art of stumbling.
The burden rained down.
It was hard work and my palms bled,
and on the backs of my hands, the slammed skin,
the punished veins rising mottled and blue.
But it was good, freeing up the newly green,
even if hopeless in those woods—the forest floor
tired and littered with the winter kill.

11.

In the animal crematorium you wait
and wait—he is a big dog
and the business of burning
is long, and his long dying day
means the night is long, because the life
he lived is long, and there is nothing to do
but pick and pick at the long white hair
covering your coat, adding it to the fistful
you cut before they took him.
A bouquet of hair you cling to,
along with the blanket deep with his smell,
and the worn collar too, the tags
that list his name with yours
biting into your palm.

The room is small, an afterthought
to harbor the waiting—the tea things, the photos
of other beloved lining the walls.
Airtight, nothing to interrupt
the fire boiling on the other side
of the concrete holding wall,
devouring the material: a maelstrom
of spit and belly and bone
that will forever keep away
unthinkable rot—

And now they come finally
with the grit and stone,

the *essence* they call it, this residue
poured in a box—with white roses
to adorn the box, for the taking away
of something so very light.
None of the heft we arranged on the table, so much
like a dog asleep on his side—
how can this be: white dog, white box
and the crossing in flames.
You are deaf with the roar, you a burned boat
bearing a stone box bearing
ashes still hot in your hands;
and you carry it with you, unbroken seal.

12.

Three days of packing and the little one has given up.
No more sad-eyed contact—pleading
look-at-me; no following
from room to room, shadowing
each move from bureau to box.
No leash at the door, no collar, no sign
she's going in the car, or that someone, anyone
might come take this stuff away, leaving them
in the house where they belong—

Underfoot, she's acted out
the question, begging for notice,
keeping herself in the way.
But now that the bed's been stripped,
she turns, leaves for another room,
pretends to hear nothing
as she finds her tossed blanket, turns round
wrapping herself, and lies down
facing the corner, the wall, fixed
on the blank, bottom space
where nothing can happen.

13.

On the cape, in the changing season,
under that noise

of sloshing against pilings, the push-in-
push-away, close then farther out;

underneath the gulls' bark, the desolate
ambient sound the dog understands—

the moving unstoppable current,
every complication reduced to repetition

as if to beat in some kind of lesson:
not urgency

in the water's fist
clenching and releasing, but *being*—

without need or purpose, and in my body all this time
the answering sweep of valves

opening and closing; just as the little
terrier, brimful of nerve and trembling,

alone, perched there, sentinel on the deck's edge,
has been trying all along to teach.

III. Essential Tremor

Magnificence, 4 AM

She thinks it wants to kill, this wind,
the wind with no mind—a transference
to everything out there.
Because she needs waking,
the howling is meant to wake her, a self
crying underneath her sleeping self,
the stilted house groaning on the edge.

For how many days now
this dominating sea?
Wind so absolute
it rides the rain sideways and up,
crashing out far beyond her
until the anchor
breaks away—
waves take possession, smash the boat
on concrete pilings.

But isn't this what she came for?

Dune Shack

To live in this place, you have to kill things.
At first you think you'll wait, you're innocent, the one
no one can blame. All those fixed
notions of what you could count on: the old life
made it possible to look the other way. But out here,
you have to deal with the obvious.
The maimed, the hopeless—
they're all around, they're waiting. Otherwise,
would your eye twitch, your right leg shake?

By the third day you've scoured the place,
but hunger being what it is, the mother mouse
moves right in, deposits her half-inch
offspring in some cotton you left unguarded.
And hearing her scratch through the night
is made worse only by her disappearance—
who knows what marsh hawk got her
or some other closer beast
foraging around the stilted shack?

So: since you're who's left, who's responsible,
Number 1, get the little things out of hiding.
Number 2, just get it over with.

Alone

The spider's long legs
more than mother
the glistening three-tiered web.
Tearing it only brings her back
resolved again, and patient—but oh
this deliberate dismantling, this person
waving a hand through it, shoving
the broken threads to the side,
brushing strands away from my face,
cursing how something still sticks
and clings, so I can't be done with it.

As if it were a plot, not a home
built with her very self. And this hunger—
this need to take all she can harvest
inside her, no end to her want—
no, how she keeps alive
is not luminous, but strict and necessary,
this moving sideways into the dark.

True Bug

I've been talking to a bug all winter.
We live together, he and I.
He's listed in the manual, oddly
wandering here from a warmer state.
His kind of insect must stay alive
all the coldest months, true bug
appearing indoors when you least expect.
But he is faultless: he will not
sting, bite, breed, eat or shit.
Mostly, he is motionless,
a long brittle shell, antennae
rarely testing the air.
His reluctant body preserves him.
I never see when he finds it necessary
to change position. He'll choose the bedpost
for a week or so, sometimes my bureau,
perched among the rings I no longer wear.
He keeps to my room with nothing
to say, no complaint to wake me.
Ours is a companionable life,
both of us going about our business—
mine bent on feeding a hungry past,
his great feat of living without.
On the first warm day, he'll know
—just like that, some screen will open.
Until then, I find him a good listener.
He doesn't mind. He waits.

Salt Water Ducks

The tide ignores its limits, all last night
climbing over the railing, battering the door.
White spume flew its ghost against the glass.
The bay's in its third day of outrage,
but the ducks have to eat. The white-winged scoter
keeps me at the window, three sleek ones.
I count the in and out of their pristine heads—
bodies down for improbable minutes
before coming back up, black and white
against the white-capped black water shoving
at the row of stone pilings that mark the tide's high rise.
By 8 a.m. I've seen enough
as the rocks submerge and the overwrought current,
something like a boxer pounding and pounding,
slams the ducks diving there— I've seen enough

to know what I'll find tomorrow on the wasted beach:
a washed-up duck, still intact,
limp sack beneath the flawless design
of its feathers, nothing odd except the crumpled pose.
Audubon propped them up on wires, a scaffold of bird—
no other way to capture life than to show it dead.
Brutality not part of art's equation, we like to think.
Meanwhile, the birds are all instinct
in the moment. This life in a wild wind
is only the din they live in. I doubt they even hear it.

Your Body Betrays You

You'd thought this place a refuge—
sand held solidly in place, all those low tides
revealing a long bar like a bridge into the sea,
seals gazing curious as dogs
as you walked out with him.
Some storm wrecked it, pointless
to say exactly when, and took the tons of sand,
moved them elsewhere.

This cold day arms itself against the season.
Knives are what you think of, water's
shards of black glass the slashing wind
throws down. Surrender is the rule: you've learned
no argument will steady your hand.

Each night your body waits out
the pill's small stay of hours.
The tide is like that—later a dark thrashing
will come back in. You push away at what's behind
this certain drowning.
Panic rides your sleep
as you try to hold steady—
your body wrestling you to the bottom.

Holding On

At breakfast on the shack's crooked stair
I look for her
in the few crossed lines
threaded by the sun, lit so lightly
as if to be ignored. From one side rail
to the other, faint white knots
catch my eye. No way to pass there
without tearing the whole creation,
and no sign of the spider—
her busy legs dragging her gossamer dress—
in whom lately I have great interest.
Where has she gone?
Into what crevice?

Bat

I don't have to wait—the evening balances on its edge
    and it comes, batting the tame light.
Here, then there, on and off in sight.
    Out of my silence, a flap,
then back in it: where did you go, little rag,
    shape of black purpose?

*

Evidence above: no begging
    wildness gone wilder or haywire
engine, no jumble in his
    darts and dives. *Don't watch me*
insisting over my head, nothing random
    and that's what I'm afraid of:

*

my longing in the 9 p.m.
    wasting light that means to tell me something
I can't deny, a frequency so high it's
    unhearable, uninventable. Pitched membrane
in that home: a dead tree
    leaning, shorn-off.

*

Avoiding it, I am drawn to it. The curse
    I fear to be there always,
even in the bright day,

upside down, hung and sleeping:
the hanged man with his unmissable clarity
is what I've made of that body—
whose job is to fly out of the dark, then return.
My job is to glimpse it.

Release

As if it were a kind of test,
you hold your body along the shallow bottom,
your slack arms dragging, openhanded.
Fingernails filling with silt, scraping the sculpted

troughs of the let-out tide, you're merely part
of the physics of the arcing rows,
each one equaling the next, this *rule* of water
meeting sand, and equally

earth's little symmetries—You remember
light scrolling through the mimosa's designs
and what your child-self saw on that grown-up fist
was a flower knocking you to the ground.

Magnet

The ocean's fickle, especially when it's cold June
and the packrat bands of ducks and gulls,
all the worse for their nipping and wailing, force themselves
on trash and more trash the winter tides kept hoisting up.
No one said *enough*. No irritable something
spoke up, nothing wanted any answers,
even when the fishing line hung from the gull's mouth
and the ribboned balloon wound itself tight
around the dead seal's neck. Now for distraction
there's all the hatching, the forward smell
of the roses' thorny mounds cutting their way
through the dunes. There is everything and nothing and why
shouldn't you see yourself the same: incidental,
without privilege, hardly meant for even this.
Consider what is indestructible: the sand's
glassy quartz, even the duller grains a semi-precious stone.
And the peppery specks? Iron, weighing it all down,
clinging as if to the bar of a magnet and buried
on the beach in beds. Think of it all
in motion, season to season, minute by minute, so that no one
who has been here, not one, occupies an actual place.

Western Conifer Seed Bug

He'd become a houseguest, noncommittal
and impassive. She tried to see to it
he wasn't disturbed, nothing to trip him up:
a book, perhaps, laid down
in some rash motion might scare him
off an edge, although he had a talent, it seemed,
for focusing on himself. He'd been so carefully
attended, she thought—warning her
guests to watch for him on the coverlet,
not over-react to his homely presence.
She kept close guard, as was her nature,
a kind of partner to help him make it
through the winter. She'd done the research
when he showed up; she knew all his business,
she had a duty. With these advantages,
how had he taken it upon himself to die?
But there he was in that trite pose,
feet in the air, as if arranged on the sink top
for her to find him. She brushed her teeth, considering
all the pine trees surrounding the house,
their heavy scent calling the half-sleeping one
at the rightful time. We were almost there—
he would have been free,
piercing and sucking that sap deep in the cones.

The Wish

Half of what I see out here I'm not sure
if I see: the whale a fantasy of whale, and what appears
to be a person's head in the incoming tide
is a trick of rocks or junk.
An arm here or there—so many
sticks, and once a hand I was sure of
became a white dog swimming off, then
just another oil can lid.

What's to believe? Dawn's silver water
whitens, a dull temper brewing
out where the bar trips the tide into frenzy.
Beyond that, a gray wall
and the sea's light is no light at all.
From this little hill, two oceans then—
close and far, but something else in an hour.

All this back and forth
reflects the knowing I try to undo:
the *not* seeing him
up on that distant dune, his descent, his figure—
moving toward me on the winding trail.

Day-Old Mice

Die, I said—coaxing, hammering
gingerly with the heel of my shoe.
Babies covered with ants, and what
has delivered them like this, alone
in plain sight on the shack's floor?
Gone ten minutes, I swear—and what
bad thing brought them out of hiding?

I was not practical, I see that now.
It is the able who must
attend the end of pain, guard
the way out of this life.
Throw me a few deaths,
and I'm shaking, revolted by the ant,
who is all mouth.
Look at him—eating his way
through whatever is necessary.

Transformation

No one likes a spider, it seems.
When my son cried out, the bite
pumping his inner elbow stiff with blood,
I did not like it either. Or the doctor,
who asked, why, if I had caught it in a glass,
had I let it go? Outside, I explained,
where it belonged. Ours was a good house,
not hospitable to anything poisonous—

•

I searched in every corner.
Lure and catch
became my manner.
I remember how my husband backed away.

•

I was in the garden,
weaving cleome's white spikes
among purple delphiniums, which had spun
their color into blue. Look
at what I've designed, I thought,
moving dirt and rocks, interlacing stones
in the raised bed. Facing inward,
I glimpsed the spider, fearing Brown Recluse:
knowing it has no home here in the north.
Had it stowed away in my bags?
Under which rock had it nested?

No longer in the house, no longer in the garden.
it found a place beneath the eaves,
protected from weather, and did its knitting.
Soon ice would hang shards
around the sealed white bundle.
No refuge for the old one, crumpled and disintegrated.
But what it had made—that gleaming knot—
kept safe until spring, the sac
billowing open, all that new life
surging forth.

New Dog

It's all about food; the world to him
is made of food. Nothing's too foreign
or remote: blackberry bushes pricking his mouth raw,
snotty tissues in the trash almost as good
as what the cat box holds. But this is trivial
as he grows, by adolescence taking up a swagger:
whatever in the face of rebuke,
arrogance to match his size. He growls.
A growl that comes from his very grounding, a starving
she can't imagine, remembering another dog's
language of kisses. His kiss is no kiss,
missing the cookie she holds too close to her face,
ripping her lip. She's bleeding, he's growling:
even cowering, he wants to eat the treat.

So she feeds him, free-feeds and feeds some more,
and still that anchor of what he is
rumbles up, a shudder
deepening in his throat, rising behind his teeth, its intent
focused in the narrowed eyes he trains on her
standing there with his bowl. So
she shoves his body back, yanks his head on both sides,
throws him down. Sideways on the floor, she straddles him
until he submits, grows limp, every threat silent inside him.
Every morning, this taming which is not a taming—
See, she says, gathering him in the sling of her arms,
her own animal self wild with *no*'s.

At Land's End

Tide out, rank odor rising
on the heated rocks. Tiny fish trapped between the boulders
dragged in from Maine, mica shining in the cracks
where my foot wavers, testing my grip
as I pause my way through, and the laughing gulls laugh.

I've made this trip out, knowing
September's full tide, the challenge to make it back
over the haphazard chain that marks
the curving tail of the cape. Once I'm there
in the deserted dunes, fresh tracks

almost turn me around, but I need
to reach the lighthouse, the white tower still beckoning,
though for years boarded-up, useless in the weeds.
Oh how I love and fear
the sprawled letters across one side: *Caterina Mollino for ever.*

Forever my own holding on—no blaming
the coyotes for sending me back to the breakwater,
or the one who is not waiting, the twenty-five years
I say goodbye to. Every brilliance
goes dark in the irony of my not seeing.

What task but to face the dead stuff
in the tide washing back, greeny detritus
hiding the barnacles, all manner of the parasitic,
because clinging is what it knows to do.
Something of balance restored,
faith in the vanishing.

Revenant

Slipped the leash, the dog's hurling down the beach,
away from water's boring lap and into the grasslands'
knee-high waves where creatures prowl or hide.
It's nearing spring: everything's a predator.
I'm thinking *lost: not now*, off the path
and chasing whatever's there into the ever-collapsing
scrub oak, split trunks, passages, holes
underground, because everything out here needs cover.

I go this way and that, screaming her foolish
human name; not a prayer she's dumb enough
to miss any cracked opening,
the telling signs of scat just outside. Foxes, coyotes,
they'll take anything into those dens.
The dog is gone, rapt with smell,
all her fifteen pounds frantic to dig, ears closed
to me—a lesser life filed under ever-faithful
same-old kibble, when there's *this*.

Reason has nowhere to take me—
feisty as she is, her gyrating tail calls up a cartoon drawing,
not ancient breeding. So I startle, caught
by a muffled barking somewhere below.
Buried, I realize, in the ground.
The dog is barking underground, resolved, insistent—
I stumble toward that fractured trail of sound
to the mouth of some fissure, and she comes
out of the earth, caked with dirt, panting,
quizzical at my panic, and in her dark eyes
everything is readable:
what now, what now?

Survival: a Guide

It's not easy living here, waiting to be charmed
by the first little scribble of green. Even in May
crows want to own the place, and the heron, old bent thing,
spends hours looking like graying bark,
part of a dead trunk lying over opaque water.
She strikes the pose so long I begin to think
she's determined to make herself into something ordinary.
The small lakes continue their slide into bog and muck—
remember when they ran clear, an invisible spring
renewing the water? But the ducks stay longer, amusing
ruffle and chatter. I can be distracted.

If I do catch her move, the heron appears
to have no particular fear or hunger, her gaunt body
hinged haphazardly, a few gears unlocking
one wing, then another. More than a generation here
and every year more drab.
Once I called her blue heron, as in Great Blue,
true to a book—part myth, part childhood's color.
Older now, I see her plain: a mere surviving
against a weedy bank with fox dens
and the ruthless, overhead patrol.
Some blind clockwork keeps her going.

Acknowledgments

Some of these poems have appeared in the following journals and magazines, sometimes in different versions or with other titles.

Five Points: "Dune Shack"
The Georgia Review: "Survival: a Guide"
Hampden-Sydney Poetry Review: "Magnet," "Noise"
The Harvard Review: "Breakwater"
The Laurel Review: "When She Spoke, He Closed His Eyes,"
        "Answer"
Michigan Quarterly Review: "In Lent," "Interstice," and "Book of
        Dog 13"
The New England Review: "Book of Dog 2," "Book of Dog 3"
The New Yorker: "Western Conifer Seed Bug"
Orion: "Bat"; "Salt Water Ducks"
Ploughshares: "Dead Fox"
Provincetown Arts: "Canis," "Chipmunk in the Pool"
The Southern Review: "Book of Dog 7," "Book of Dog 12"
City: "Ants Want My Yellow Moth," "Holding On" (as
        "Disguise")
Plume: "True Bug"
Poetry Bay: "Book of Dog 1" (as "Aubade"), "Book of Dog 8"

"Canis" was published in *The Best American Poetry 2009*.
"Survival: a Guide" was featured on *Poetry Daily*.
"I Will Be Good" appeared in *The Plume Anthology of Poetry 2013*.

Notes

The book's epigraph is from *Crow With No Mouth* by Ikkyū, translated from the Japanese by Stephen Berg.

"Book of Dog 7" is for Michael Savage.
"Book of Dog 11" is for Alexandra Mathis.
"New Dog" is for Martha Rhodes.
Mary Holland's essays in *Naturally Curious* were the inspiration for *True Bug* and *Western Conifer Seed Bug*.

I am most grateful for frequent poetry fellowships from the Corporation of Yaddo, where most of these poems were written, and to the Peaked Hill Trust, where time in the dune shacks on Cape Cod inspired the poems into being. I also wish to thank the Brown Family Foundation at the Museum of Fine Arts for a generous fellowship in the Dora Maar House in Provence, France.

I appreciate Dartmouth College's support, especially the 2009–10 sabbatical, which I devoted to this work.

Dear friends and family whose help and encouragement was immeasurable include Zack Finch, Pamela Harrison, Gary Lenhart, Martha Rhodes, Darsie Riccio, Sara Warner-Phillips, and Martha Webster, as well as Simon, Tessa, Alexandra, and Zachary.

CLEOPATRA MATHIS was born and raised in Ruston, Louisiana. The author of six books of poems, her work has appeared widely in anthologies, textbooks, magazines and journals, including *The New Yorker, Poetry, Ploughshares, TriQuarterly, The Southern Review, The Georgia Review, The Made Thing: An Anthology of Contemporary Southern Poetry,* and *The Extraordinary Tide: Poetry by American Women.* Prizes for her work include two National Endowment for the Arts grants, the Jane Kenyon Award, the Peter I. B. Lavan Younger Poets Award, two Pushcart Prizes, the Robert Frost Award, and fellowships from the Fine Arts Work Center in Provincetown, Massachusetts, the New Hampshire State Council on the Arts, and the New Jersey State Arts Council. Mathis is the Frederick Sessions Beebe '35 Professor in the Art of Writing at Dartmouth College.

Sarabande Books thanks you for the purchase of this book; we do hope you enjoy it! Founded in 1994 as an independent, nonprofit, literary press, Sarabande publishes poetry, short fiction, and literary nonfiction—genres increasingly neglected by commercial publishers. We are committed to producing beautiful, lasting editions that honor exceptional writing, and to keeping those books in print. If you're interested in further reading, take a moment to browse our website, www.sarabandebooks.org. There you'll find information about other titles; opportunities to contribute to the Sarabande mission; and an abundance of supporting materials including audio, video, a lively blog, and our Sarabande in Education program.